John Deere, That's Who!

Tracy Nelson Maurer

Illustrated by Tim Zeltner

HENRY HOLT AND COMPANY
NEW YORK

Henry Holt and Company, LLC
Publishers since 1866
175 Fifth Avenue, New York, New York 10010
mackids.com

Library of Congress Cataloging-in-Publication Data
Names: Maurer, Tracy, 1965– author. | Zeltner, Tim, illustrator.
Title: John Deere, that's who! / Tracy Nelson Maurer ; illustrated by Tim Zeltner.
Description: First edition. | New York : Henry Holt and Company, 2017. |
    Includes bibliographical references.
Identifiers: LCCN 2016002105 | ISBN 9781627791298 (hardcover)
Subjects: LCSH: Deere, John, 1804–1886—Juvenile literature. | Deere &
    Company—History—Juvenile literature. | Plows—History—Juvenile literature.
Classification: LCC CT275.D3256 M38 2017 | DDC 338.7/6817631092—dc23
LC record available at http://lccn.loc.gov/2016002105

Our books may be purchased in bulk for promotional, educational, or business use. Please
contact your local bookseller or the Macmillan Corporate and Premium Sales Department
at (800) 221-7945 ext. 5442 or by e-mail at MacmillanSpecialMarkets@macmillan.com.

First Edition—2017 / Designed by Liz Dresner
The illustrations for this book were created using acrylic on plywood and a unique
combination of stains and glazes.
Printed in China by RR Donnelley Asia Printing Solutions Ltd., Dongguan City,
Guangdong Province

10 9 8 7 6 5 4 3 2 1

For Mike, my favorite

—T. N. M.

To Liam

—T. Z.

*B*ack in John Deere's day, long before tractors and other newfangled contraptions, Americans dug the land with the same kind of plow that farmers had used as long as anyone could remember.

That plow in the 1830s was surely less than perfect. But it worked.

So, who would want to change it?

John Deere, that's who.

But John
didn't set out
to build a new
plow right away.
He was just another
young blacksmith from Vermont—
a hardworking one, mind you. His fine skills
earned him buckets of praise. Still, times were tough, and
folks sometimes failed to pay him. John's business struggled.

Then disaster struck. His forge burned to the ground.

'Course, John rebuilt it.

And then—another fire!

Soon he was out of cash and out of luck.

John needed a fresh start. So, with a few of his best ironworking tools, he joined the stream of pioneers headed west in 1836.

He planned to send for his wife and
children when he was settled.

Luck started to shine on him when he arrived in Grand Detour, Illinois. The little town needed a blacksmith to fix broken pots and pans, horseshoes and pitchforks, and shovels and plows—lots and lots of plows.

John quickly built a forge. Smoke poured from the slow fire that burned from sunrise to sunset, and sometimes longer than that.

Clang!

Clang!

Clang!

That man was a workhorse, hammering red-hot iron to repair tools so they were as good as new— even better than new!

John also fixed the farmers' heavy iron plows.

Again.

And again.

Stubborn, twisted roots deep under the prairie banged up the iron blades. Even worse, the thick, rich soil the farmers called gumbo (in a not-so-nice way) stuck to their plows like gummy black snowballs. Farmers had to stop every so often to scrape the gumbo off with a paddle. That made a day's work take a lot longer.

John heard the farmers complain again and again.

I reckon I'm cleanin' that plow pret' near ev'ry few steps.

It's a-gone take me forev'r and a day to plow my claim.

Uff-da! This heavy plow wrenches the dickens outta my back!

They were tuckered out.
Some farmers talked about hightailing it back east, where the soil was sandy and easy to till.
John didn't want to lose his customers.
Truth be told, he missed his family. And he had a debt to pay.

That's when John set his mind to building a better plow.

He tried new plow angles.

He studied how the gumbo clung to the tiny pits in the iron.

It's a fair guess that John already knew of other plow designs that called for lightweight steel rather than heavy iron.

But steel was rare that far west and too pricey.

Then one day at the sawmill in 1837, John found
a broken steel saw blade that he could take back to
his smithy. There, John chiseled off the saw's teeth
and cut the steel into the shape of a plow's blade.

He curved it over a log so it would shrug off soil. Then he polished the steel as shiny as his mother's sewing needles. Those needles could slip through calico like a hot knife through butter.

Maybe a shiny plow would slice through gumbo.

The town's families gathered at a local farmer's
field to watch John test his gleaming "self-polisher."
They didn't expect much.
But who amazed them all?

John Deere, that's who.

Stories of the day claimed he dug twelve rows, neat as you please!

Many farmers were still leery.

John built several plows for farmers to try in their own fields.

Test after test, John's smooth steel plow cut so quickly and easily, it truly hummed down the rows. In time, customers began asking for Mr. Deere's "singing plow."

You can bet John was happy to send for his family in 1838—and mighty relieved to settle his debt five years later.

In another five years, the entire Deere family moved to Moline, Illinois. John wanted his company closer to the Mississippi River for better waterpower and easier deliveries.

All the while, John kept tinkering with the plow design to keep his customers happy.

Under his leadership, John's company sold tens of thousands of singing plows and other horse-drawn equipment.

Farmers plowed the prairie soil faster than ever. They planted more than enough food for their families, selling the extra crops. Farming grew into a business.

And the prairie's fields of grain became known as America's breadbasket.

So, who changed the plow for America's farmers?

Who changed a nation forever?

John Deere, that's who!

GLOSSARY

calico — A heavy cotton cloth used for dresses, curtains, and other items in the 1700s and 1800s.

debt — Money owed to someone or to a bank.

forge — The workplace of a blacksmith. It also means the fireplace, or hearth, where the blacksmith heats the metal.

smithy — Another name for a forge, where a blacksmith works on metal. It also refers to the person who works in the forge.

steel — A mix of iron and carbon that is usually heated to a liquid, then poured into sheets that are rolled flat. Unlike iron or cast iron, steel can keep a sharp edge and becomes smooth and shiny when polished.

till — To dig the soil and make it ready for planting, or to pull weeds.

DIG INTO MORE FACTS ABOUT
JOHN DEERE AND HIS COMPANY

JOHN DEERE
February 7, 1804–May 17, 1886

- John Deere wasn't the first American to tinker with plow designs. Before he became president, Thomas Jefferson sketched plans in 1788 for a new plow to turn the soil on his hilly plantation. Others, such as Jethro Wood in 1819, tried cast-iron designs for plows with replaceable parts. But John was the first to blend the best ideas about plow designs and steel parts to make a better tool for America's thick prairie soil.

- Many farmers who used wooden plows in the 1830s believed iron or steel would poison the soil. John let them test his steel plow in their fields to show it was safe.

- Before John Deere, most blacksmiths made plows one at a time as farmers placed their orders. Deere & Company offered ready-made plows and sold them in "branch houses" across the Midwest. Pioneers bought their self-polishers at these stores as they traveled on their westward journey.

- John Deere was the mayor of Moline for two years after he retired.

- John Deere never lived on a farm.

- John Deere didn't invent the tractor. He died thirty-two years before his company bought the Waterloo Gasoline Engine Company and began selling the Waterloo Boy Model R—the granddaddy of all John Deere tractors.

- Deere & Company has sold carriages, wagons, and even bicycles in addition to plows and other farm equipment. Today, it's one of America's oldest manufacturing companies.

BIBLIOGRAPHY

JOHN DEERE was not much of a writer. He didn't keep a diary or jot notes about his work. He preferred talking with folks in person.

Much of what historians have documented about this American manufacturing icon comes from the recollections of family and friends, notes in diaries, newspaper articles, letters, and business materials. The sources used to create this book are listed here.

Alm, Diana. *John Deere, the Man Who Opened the Prairie.* Moline, IL: Illinois Writers' Guild, 1985.

Beemer, Rod, and Tracy Nelson Maurer. *John Deere.* St. Paul: Motorbooks, 2006.

Broehl Jr., Wayne G. *John Deere's Company: A History of Deere & Company and Its Times.* New York: Doubleday and Company, 1984.

Calkins, Earnest Elmo. *They Broke the Prairie: Being some account of the settlement of the Upper Mississippi Valley by religious and educational pioneers, told in terms of one city, Galesburg, and of one college, Knox.* New York: Charles Scribner's Sons, 1937.

Clark, Neil M. *John Deere: He Gave to the World the Steel Plow.* Moline, IL: Desaulniers & Company, 1937.

Collins, David R. *Pioneer Plowmaker: A Story about John Deere.* Minneapolis: Lerner Publishing Group, 1990.

Dahlstrom, Neil, and Jeremy Dahlstrom. *The John Deere Story: A Biography of Plowmakers John and Charles Deere.* DeKalb, IL: Northern Illinois University Press, 2005.

Historic Rock Island County: History of the Settlement of Rock Island County from the Earliest Known Period to the Present Time. Rock Island, IL: Kramer & Company, 1908.

Kendall, Edward C. *John Deere's Steel Plow.* United States National Museum, Bulletin 218, Smithsonian Institution, Washington, DC, 1959, pp. 15–25. The Project Gutenberg EBook: gutenberg.org/files/34562/34562-h/34562-h.htm#Page_17.

Macmillan, Don, ed. *The John Deere Tractor Legacy: The Complete Illustrated History from Tractors & Machinery to Deere's Role in Farm Life, 1837 to Today.* Stillwater, MN: Voyageur Press, 2003.

The Moline Workman. "A Stroll About Town." November 29, 1854.

Pierce, Bess. *Moline: A Pictorial History.* Virginia Beach, VA: Donning Company, 1981.

Sutcliffe, Jane. *John Deere.* History Maker Bios. Minneapolis: Lerner Publications, 2007.

For more information about John Deere and his company, visit the John Deere website, deere.com.

ACKNOWLEDGMENTS

I GREW UP near Superior, Wisconsin, in the country but not on a farm. My friends drove tractors, milked cows, and stacked hay bales. They taught me to appreciate the farming heritage in America. When I learned about John Deere's legacy, I was excited to share his story.

Many people helped me with this book, including Rick Trahan, master blacksmith at the John Deere homesite in Grand Detour, Illinois; Neil Dahlstrom, archivist for Deere & Company in Moline, Illinois; the John Deere Pavilion docents in Moline; and the helpful (and patient) public librarians in Moline and Minneapolis. I extend my deep appreciation to Ann Matzke, Joyce Sidman, Laura Purdie Salas, Mary Bevis, Tunie Munson-Benson, Michelle Lackner, Claire Rudolf Murphy, and my other dear friends and family (especially Mike, Meg, and Tommy) who supported this long process. I'm also grateful to Kendra Marcus and the BookStop Literary crew, Sally Doherty and the Henry Holt team, and the Hamline University MFA Program in Writing for Children and Young Adults. Any misinterpretations or mistakes were inadvertent and mine alone.

I'm glad you could dig into John Deere with me!

—T. N. M.